To: Jillian + Justin + Annie
I hope this book inspires your c[...]

BENJAMIN AND THE BACKYARD BEAST

By Erin Lee

Illustrated by Abira Das

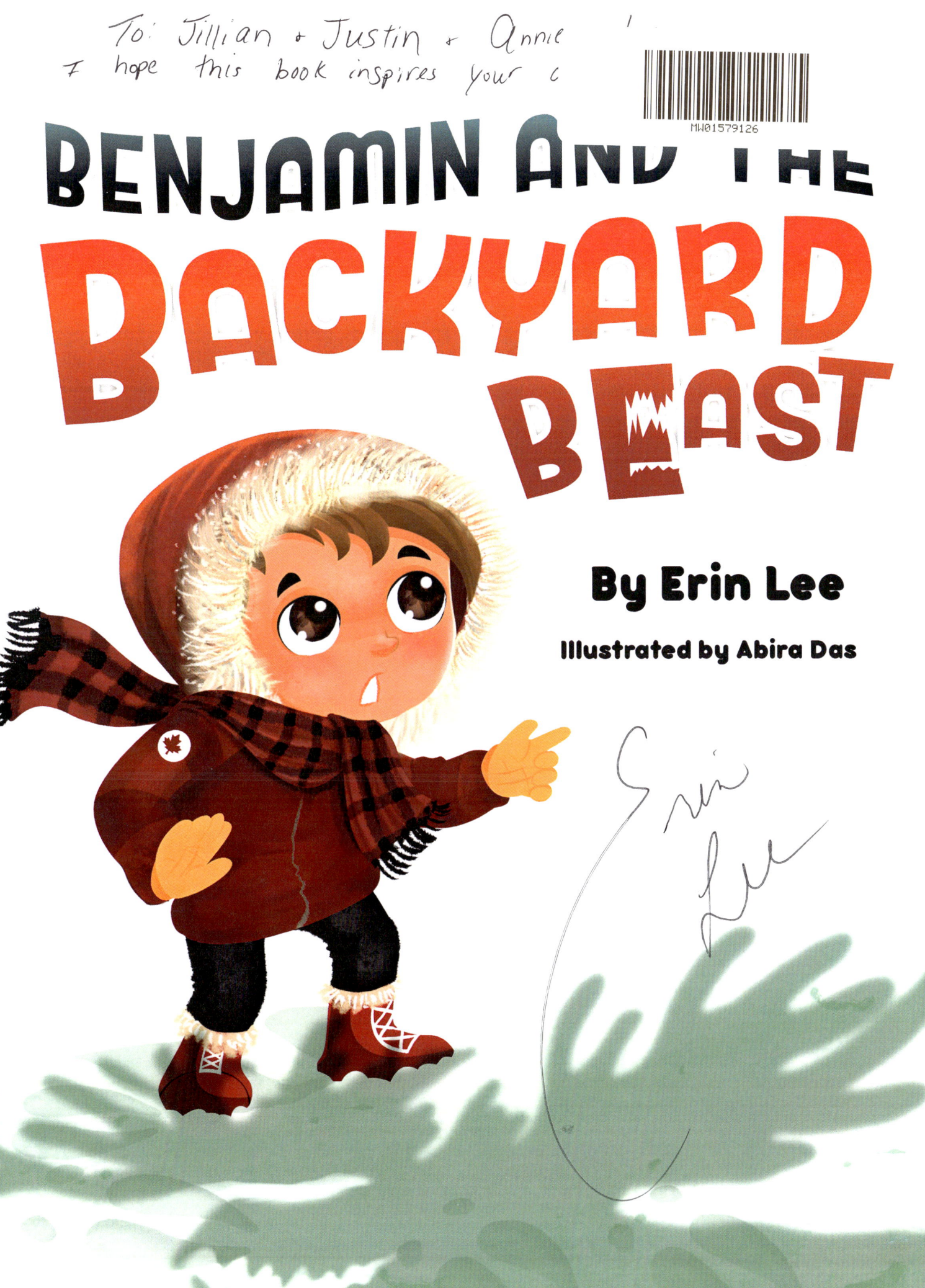

BENJAMIN AND THE BACKYARD BEAST

BENJAMIN AND THE BACKYARD BEAST © 2022 ERIN LEE

Written by : Erin Lee
Illustrated by : Abira Das

Published by Sunset Press

All rights reserved. This book or parts thereof may
not be reproduced in any form, stored in a retrieval system, or
transmitted in any form by any means—electronic, mechanical,
photocopy, recording, or otherwise—
without prior written permission of the publisher.

ISBN: 978-1-7775351-6-2

Land Acknowledgement

I, Erin Lee, as well as my publishing team, would like to acknowledge that the setting in this book (Saint Lawrence River Valley, Ontario) is situated on the homeland of the Kanien'kehá:ka (People of the Flint) Nation, also known as the Mohawk Nation. The Kanien'kehá:ka, or Mohawk, is one of the five founding nations of the Haudenosaunee Confederacy, who were referred to as the "Eastern Door."

With gratitude and respect, we acknowledge the significant contributions Indigenous Peoples have made and continue to make. We will continue to restore and develop our relationship with the First Nations, Métis, and Inuit Peoples with whom we share this land. In pursuing our commitment to restoring this relationship, is it important that, in addition to recognizing that we are situated on the homelands of Indigenous Peoples, we also learn about and honour their cultures.

For more information on how you can spread awareness, we invite you to see the bonus pack in this book, which contains a component written by the Native North American Travelling College and the Akwesasne Freedom School in Akwesasne, New York. I sincerely thank these organizations for their knowledge and effort in the creation of this significant part of the book.

Benjamin and the Backyard Beast is a true story about my own Canadian childhood, in which I shared a love of nature (and moose searching) with my father. I am so thankful for the ability to live and make these special memories on this land. I ask that you join me in thanking those who have lived here for millennia and have taken care of, and continue to take care of, this beautiful land on which we live.

For every book purchased, a portion of proceeds are donated to the Akwesasne Freedom School.

This book is dedicated to my dad, who took me on adventures in our backyard, and introduced me to my very first "backyard beast" (moose).

Little home, quiet home, warm as could be.
Mama and I had just put on some tea.

Baby was sleeping, and Daddy was out.
I sat there so restless, my face in a pout.

"Mama, oh Mama, let's go out to play.
I'm stuck in this house on this snowy, white day!"

"Benjamin, Benjamin, wipe off that frown.
It's too cold outside, and the sun's going down."

Just then, from outside, came a startling blow.

Daddy burst through the door
and shook off the snow.

"Daddy, oh Daddy!
You're back from the trail!

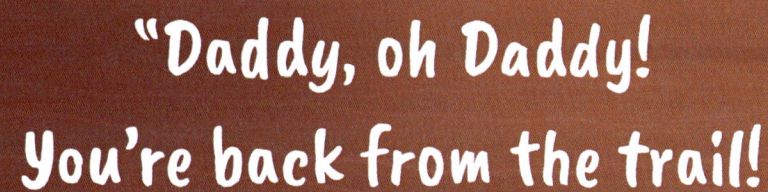

What did you see?
Give me every detail!"

"Daddy, oh Daddy,
just what have you seen?
What is this beast?
Is it scary or mean?"

"Bye, Mama! Bye, baby," we called as we fled.
I held on so tightly as Dad pulled my sled.

The air hit my cheeks, and...

the cold bit my toes,

but I wanted to come so I kept my mouth closed.

"Benjamin, Benjamin, look up ahead!
It's brown and it's small, and it wants to be fed."
I glanced up the trail, and I squinted to see.
"That's not a moose! But what could it be?"

So onwards we went, on our quest to unveil the backyard beast of the trees and the trail.

"Benjamin, Benjamin, look down this way!
It's got a black mask and its body is grey."

I stared at the creature.
It gazed back at me.

"That's not a moose, so what do I see?"
"Raccoon, oh raccoon, the footprints you make aren't those of a moose—there is no mistake!"

So onwards we went, on our quest to unveil the backyard beast of the trees and the trail.

"Benjamin, Benjamin, look over there! The quills and the droppings were left everywhere."

I watched where Dad pointed, and then in the tree
I saw something moving, but what could it be?

"Daddy, oh Daddy, a big porcupine!
It's sure not a moose,
'cause a moose doesn't climb."

So onwards we went, on our quest to unveil the backyard beast of the trees and the trail.

"Benjamin, Benjamin,
look to the sky!
Now hold out your hand,
and it might just pass by."

I peered up above as the little bird flew.
"You're not a moose, so what, then, are you?"

"Chickadee, chickadee, check out your wings. A moose wouldn't have such feathery things."

So onwards we went, on our quest to unveil the backyard beast of the trees and the trail.

"Benjamin, Benjamin, look at that wall! . What sort of creature built something so tall?"

The river was ice,
a clear sheet of glass,
but beneath it I saw
something swimming, quite fast!

"Beaver, oh beaver,
your tail's much too wide
to be that of a moose,
so just go back and hide!"

So onwards we went, on our quest to unveil the backyard beast of the trees and the trail. "Benjamin, Benjamin, look at that den! This animal sleeps 'til it's warm out again."

I stared into the darkness, and managed to spy three cubs and their mama, asleep, safe and dry.

The searching went on, but the sun was now low, and the cold hit me hard from my head to my toe.

"Forest, oh forest,
where could our beast be?
You've swallowed the moose
that we so long to see."

"Benjamin, Benjamin, let's turn around.
We'll come back tomorrow and look 'til it's found."
My head dropped in defeat and I held in a cry.
Then I studied the forest and waved it goodbye.

But just as we turned
to start venturing back
I heard a faint snap
echo far down the track.

A dark silhouette
pressed against the pink sky,
standing still like a painting,
its large head held high.

With a lump in my throat
and a knot in my belly,
I shut my eyes tight
as my legs turned to jelly.

We watched it in silence, and I'll never forget the most impressive beast I ever have met.

But beast is a word that is sadly misused, for this giant was gentle, and beautiful too.

Its legs seemed to go on for miles and miles!
I looked toward Dad, who flashed a big smile.

A machine of pure muscle, a creature of power.
How long were we out there? One minute? One hour?

A mystical snapshot, that didn't last long.
In the blink of an eye, the big beast was gone.

We went home in silence.
Our hearts were content.
And when we got back,
Mama asked where we went.

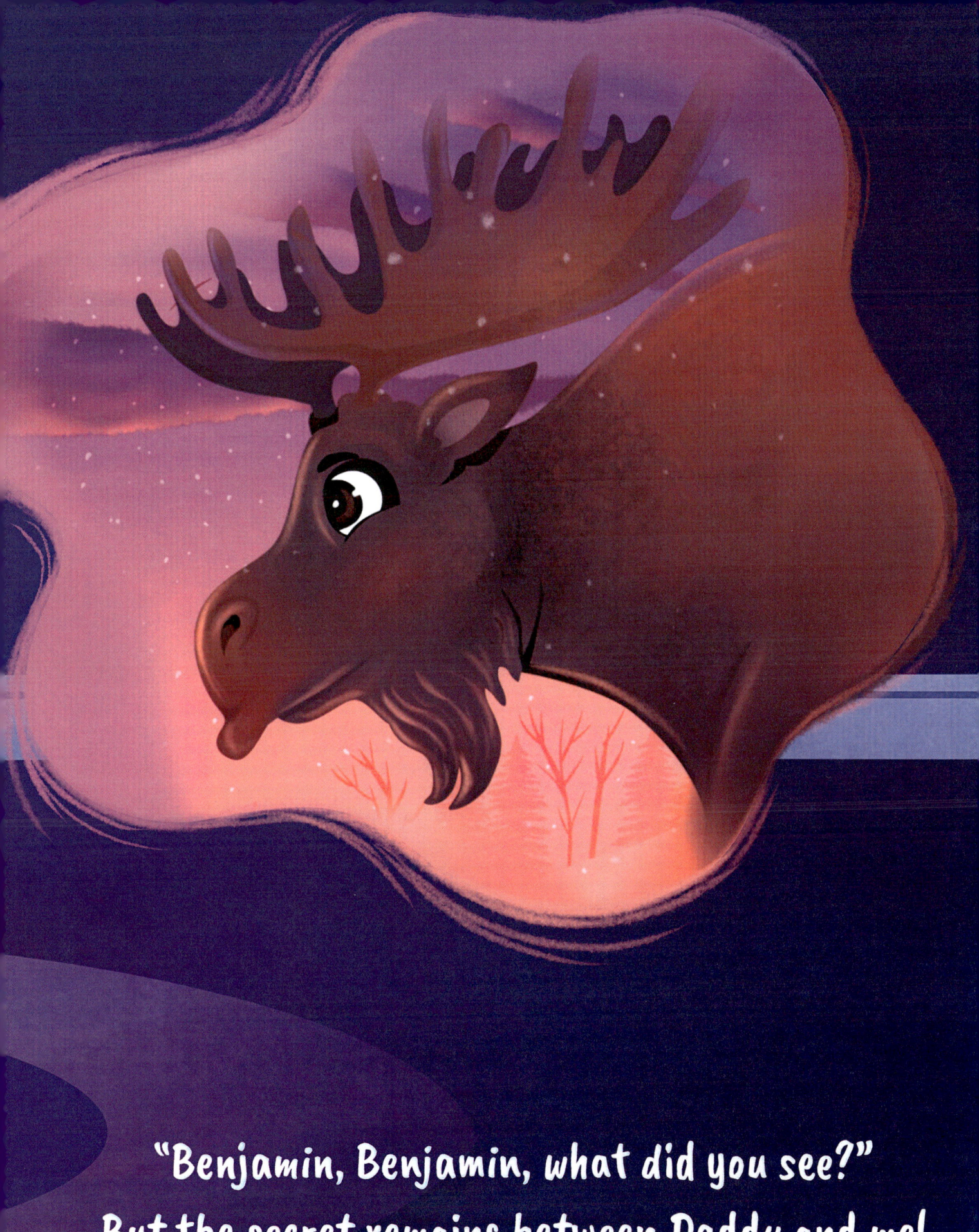

"Benjamin, Benjamin, what did you see?"
But the secret remains between Daddy and me!

Let's Learn Some Vocabulary!

Herbivore – An animal that eats only plants.

Carnivore – An animal that eats only other animals (meat).

Omnivore – An animal that eats plants and other animals (meat).

Hibernation – Hibernation is a state when an animal is inactive during the cold winter months. When animals hibernate, they find a safe place and stay there until the end of winter. While they are hibernating, their body temperature falls drastically and they barely breathe. Not all animals hibernate. Read the animal facts at the back of this book to find out which animals in this story do.

Nocturnal – Animals that are active at night are called nocturnal. Nocturnal animals look for food at night and sleep or hide during the day.

Diurnal – Animals that are active during the day are called diurnal. Diurnal animals look for food during the day and sleep or rest at night.

Endangered – When an animal species is endangered, it means there are not many of them left in the world. An animal species can become endangered when too many of them are hunted by humans or other animals or when their habitats are destroyed.

Mammal – Mammals include humans and other animals who have a backbone and breathe air. All mammals have hair or fur at some point in their lives (even dolphins have hair, when they are first born!). They feed their young with milk and they are warm-blooded. Mammals are born live, not from eggs.

Learn About the Animals from Benjamin and the Backyard Beast

  Squirrel

There are 22 different species of squirrels living in Canada, including flying squirrels. Some squirrels live in trees and some on the ground. The squirrel that we saw in this story is called a bushy-tailed squirrel (also known as the Sciurus). It is active all year round, but other common ground squirrels hibernate during the winter.

A squirrel's tail is a very useful tool. It can keep the squirrel warm during cold nights and can also provide shade during warmer weather.

While different species of squirrels have different kinds of diets, most squirrels are herbivores. This means that they eat seeds, nuts, acorns, and berries. Most squirrels, including bushy-tailed squirrels, are diurnal, or active during the day, but flying squirrels are nocturnal.

   Raccoon

The most common type of raccoon is the Procyon lotor, and it typically has a grey body and a black mask. Raccoons are found in many areas of North America. They can live in a variety of habitats, as long as their basic needs for water, food, and shelter are met. They often find shelter in dens in swamps, forests, or marshes. Raccoons do not hibernate in the winter. They build up body fat in the fall and then, when food is scarce, they conserve their energy through a period called inactivity, when they sleep in their dens. Every few weeks, they come out of the den to look for food. The raccoon in Benjamin and the Backyard Beast was doing exactly that: searching for food!

Raccoons are omnivores and will eat just about anything they can find, including seeds, plants, leaves, and berries (or anything in your garbage, if they can get to it!).

Porcupine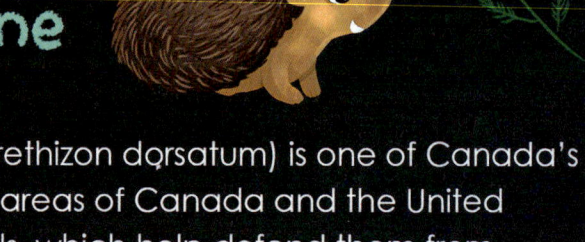

The North American porcupine (called the Erethizon dorsatum) is one of Canada's best known mammals. Porcupines live in different areas of Canada and the United States. They can be recognized by their sharp quills, which help defend them from enemies in the forest. A porcupine has over 30 000 quills—that's a lot of little needles! When it meets an enemy, a porcupine can lose a few hundred quills while trying to defend itself, and it will use its tail to sink the needles into the other animal.

Porcupines live in dens or in trees. Sometimes you have to look closely, because they are not always easy to find. The best way to spot a porcupine is to look for droppings and quills under trees. When they are not hiding in trees, they can be found in their dens (in rock piles or caves).

Porcupines do not hibernate during the winter. In colder months, they take shelter in their dens or trees, sleeping a lot of the time and finding food nearby. Porcupines are herbivores, and they eat bark as well as plants. They are nocturnal animals.

Chickadee

Four different types of chickadees live in Canada: the black-capped chickadee, the mountain chickadee, the boreal chickadee, and the chestnut-backed chickadee. The most common one in Canada is the black-capped chickadee (also called Poecileatricapilla). It has a grey body, a white belly, and a black "cap" on its head. These birds are known for their call, which sounds like they are saying chickadee-dee-dee. In the fall and winter, black-capped chickadees live in flocks of four to twelve birds. The flock sticks together, flying from tree to tree in one distinct area. They take shelter among branches or in bushy spruces.

In the winter, chickadees do not hibernate or fly south. Instead, they eat more food on a regular basis to keep their energy levels up during the cold nights. They can also lower their body temperature at night to save their energy.

Chickadees are diurnal, or most active during the day. They spend most of their time searching for food. They are omnivorous animals, eating a variety of insects, berries, seeds, and spiders. During the warmer months, they gather food and hide it in a small space. Chickadees can remember the location of their hidden food for up to 28 days!

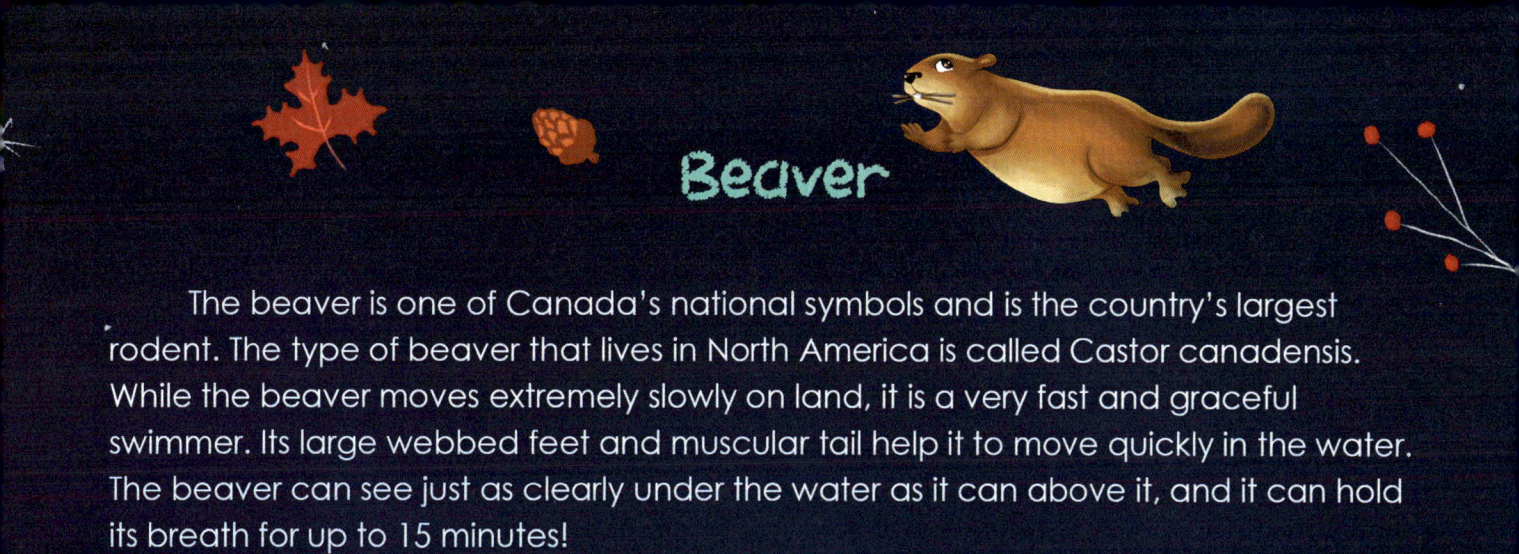

Beaver

    The beaver is one of Canada's national symbols and is the country's largest rodent. The type of beaver that lives in North America is called Castor canadensis. While the beaver moves extremely slowly on land, it is a very fast and graceful swimmer. Its large webbed feet and muscular tail help it to move quickly in the water. The beaver can see just as clearly under the water as it can above it, and it can hold its breath for up to 15 minutes!

    Beavers are amazing builders. They use their strong, flexible tails to balance when they stand upright on their hind legs. This is especially helpful when they are carrying building materials, such as mud, stones, or branches, with their front paws. While beavers typically build habitats called lodges, their best-known structures are dams. A beaver builds a dam when it needs to expand the underwater area it will live in for the winter. The dam creates a deep pond that will not freeze all the way to the bottom, so the beaver can swim under the ice. The beaver builds its lodge into the ice and over the water's surface so it can stay dry when it's inside. This is exactly what we saw in Benjamin and the Backyard Beast! Beavers prepare for the winter by gathering food in a pile directly in their pond. This food pile is called a cache. During the winter, they swim back and forth under the ice, taking food from the cache and bringing it to their lodge to eat.

    Beavers do not hibernate during the winter. At times, they will surface for some extra food, but they normally enjoy being sheltered during the colder months. Beavers are herbivores, eating herbs, grasses, various trees, and fruits. Although they can be spotted during the day, they are usually nocturnal, doing most of their building at night.

Black Bear

The black bear (also called the Ursus americanus) is one of three bear species found in North America (along with the grizzly bear and polar bear). In Canada, the black bear can be spotted in most provinces, particularly in British Columbia. It has round ears, small eyes, and a very small tail. A black bear's large feet allows it to walk on its hind legs (like a human!) or climb trees. Its strong claws are the perfect tool for digging holes and searching for food.

The average male black bear weighs about 135 kilograms (or 298 pounds). Compare that to the average human weight of a thirty-year-old male in Canada, just 75 kilograms (or 167 pounds)!

Black bears live in forest areas and take shelter in dens (caves, rocks, and large holes). When the temperature begins to drop in autumn, they eat more food to prepare for the winter.

Black bears and grizzlies are not true hibernators. When an animal hibernates, its body temperature drops drastically. However, the black bear's temperature only drops by a few degrees. While they aren't technically hibernating, it may look like they are! This is because their heart rate and breathing slow down, and they become slower and sleepier. During warmer periods in winter, some black bears might wake up and wander for a short time before returning to sleep.

Black bears are omnivores and will eat just about anything available to them. While they mostly eat plants and berries, they prey on other mammals, insects, and salmon. Black bears are active during the night and the day, and they take frequent naps.

Moose

Finally, our "backyard beast"—the moose! Moose (also called Alces alces) can be found in different parts of the world, including Europe, Asia, and North America. There are four subspecies of moose in North America: the Alaskan moose, the northwestern moose, the eastern moose, and the Shiras moose. All four species can be spotted in different regions of Canada.

The moose stands as tall as 2 metres (or 6.5 feet), which is taller than most humans! It is the largest of all the deer species. Male moose have large antlers, while females do not.

Moose usually live near water (lakes, rivers, and streams) in the forest. They are very good swimmers and will often swim to find aquatic plants to eat or to help them stay cool in the summer. In the winter, moose do not hibernate. Instead, they look for forests with less snow so they can find food more easily.

Moose are herbivores, eating pinecones, branches, and plants. Since they are tall, they prefer to find their food in higher areas, such as in tall shrubs and higher grasses. Using their hooves, they scrape snow away to get to the moss on the ground. While moose are mostly diurnal animals (active during the day), they are especially active at dawn and dusk. This is probably why the characters in Benjamin and the Backyard Beast did not spot the moose until the end of the day!

Over the years, the moose population has become threatened. In Canada, the development of homes and cities has destroyed many forests, causing many moose to lose their habitat. While the number of moose is still high in some provinces, they are endangered in others. To find out more about how you can help, visit www.natureconservancy.ca.

An Introduction to the Haudenosaunee

The Haudenosaunee are Indigenous people of the Northeast who built longhouse dwellings in the past and continue to use longhouses for ceremonies and meetings today. Our traditional form of democratic government has continued to exist for a millennium under the Great Law of Peace. Currently, the Haudenosaunee Confederacy includes the Kanien'kehá:ka (Mohawk) Nation, Oneida Nation, Onondaga Nation, Cayuga Nation, Seneca Nation, and Tuscarora Nation. Our philosophies and teachings are based on Peace, Respect, and using a Good Mind to give thanks for all that our Creator has given us. Taking care of the resources that our land, waters, and air share with us all is a primary responsibility given to our people since the beginning of time. These teachings need to be strengthened among all people on Turtle Island.
-Iakonikonriiosta
Native North American Traveling College Manager

The Akwesasne Freedom School has provided Mohawk translations for each of the animals in the story. I, Erin Lee, sincerely thank the Akwesasne Freedom School for their contribution to this part of the book.

    I would also like to extend my deepest gratitude for these animals, who lived in the forest of my backyard.

    The animal artwork displayed on the next page is by Bruce Boots, an artist from Akwesasne. He has depicted his view of each animal in the book and explains his work in this way: "The graphics depict our skydomes with celestial trees at the top of the domes. The triangular designs on the bodies are designs that we use in pottery and beadwork borders. The spirals are an element that can be water, wind, or a journey to the center. These are all elements that are used in our beadwork patterns."

For more information on the Haudenosaunee, visit these websites:
Haudenosaunee Confederacy: www.haudenosauneeconfederacy.com
Onondaga Nation: www.onondaganation.org
Native Land Digital: www.native-land.ca

Chickadee
Tsiktsiré:re - It is the literal sound they make (just as the English word represents the sound they make)

Black Bear
Wahkwari'tahòn:tsi - It is made of black fur

Squirrel
Onkwe'tá:kon - They live around people

Moose
Ska'niónhsa - Big nose

Beaver
Wani'tonnién:nis - They make mounds/dams

Porcupine
Anéntaks - It eats the bark

Racoon
Raiá:tes - It has a long body

Can you find the following objects in the book?

Squirrel nest 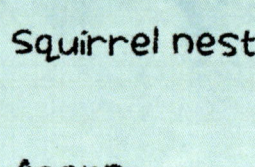	Maple trees 	Spruce
Acorn 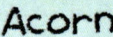	Skates 	Cedar 
Snow shoes	Lacrosse stick	Pine 
Fisherman 	Hockey Stick	Hemlock 
Feather	Canadian flag 	Red Twig Dogwood 
Maple syrup 	Fir 	Winter Berries 

Which footprint belongs to which animal?

Write the correct answer on each line below.

_____ _____ _____

_____ _____ _____

Can you answer the following questions about the story?

1. What is your favourite animal from the story and why?
2. In the story, why do you think Benjamin and his father decided not to tell the rest of their family about the moose?
3. How many quills can a porcupine have?
4. What are baby bears called?
5. How many different types of squirrels are found in Canada?
6. Do raccoons hibernate in the winter?
7. What do herbivores eat?
8. Which of the animals in the story is one of Canada's national symbols?
9. What does it mean for an animal to be endangered?
10. Why are moose becoming endangered in some parts of Canada?
11. What do you think Benjamin and his father will do next?

For more information about these animals and how you can protect them, check out these websites!

Orkin Canada's library of pests: www.orkincanada.ca/pests

Hinterland Who's Who: www.hww.ca

Nature Conservancy of Canada: www.natureconservancy.ca

National Geographic's animal information: www.kids.nationalgeographic.com/animals

Erin Lee is a teacher with the Upper Canada District School Board. She lives in Long Sault, Ontario. Growing up, she loved exploring her Canadian surroundings, playing sports, and spending time with her family. Now she loves writing about these experiences.

After finishing her bachelor of fine arts and bachelor of education, Erin began teaching elementary school. When she's not busy getting messy with her thirty kindergarteners, she's writing stories about them—and for them! Erin's stories have grown into three highly praised published children's books: Maggie the Magnificent, Out Of Season, and, most recently, Benjamin and the Backyard Beast.

Erin has recently launched a line of unique products based on her books. She enjoys leading workshops and designing teaching products for educators to use in their own classrooms. Through her work, Erin aims to raise awareness about important lessons based on social skills, life skills, and academics. She hopes that her stories will spark a love of reading and inspire younger generations to be the best humans they can be.

IF YOU LIKED THIS BOOK DO CHECK OUT

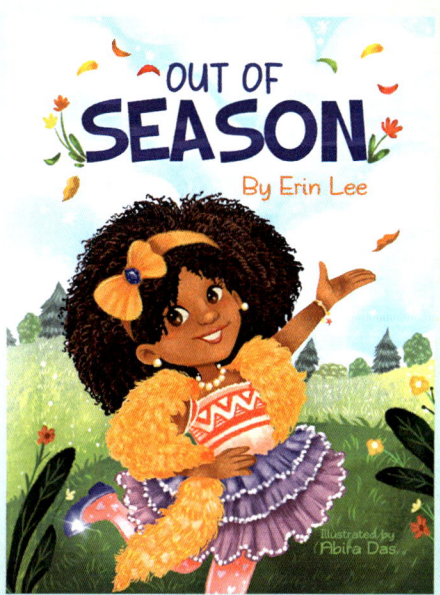

Follow "Erin Lee" on Social media to grab free teaching resources that accompany her books!

www.erinleeauthor.com

- info@erinleeauthor.com
- www.instagram.com/erin.lee.author/
- www.facebook.com/authorerinlee/
- www.teacherspayteachers.com/Store/Erin-Lee-Author